WITHDRAWN

MODEL DESIGN
AND BUILDING

OY SCOUTS OF AMERICA
VING, TEXAS

Requirements

1. Study and understand the requirements for personal safety when using such modelmaker hand tools as knives, scissors, handsaws, scratch awl, files, hammer, screwdriver, hand drills and drill bits, pliers, and wire cutters. Know what precautions to take when using flammable or hazardous products such as glue, epoxy, paint, and thinners, and proper protective equipment such as goggles to be used when grinding or drilling. Discuss these with your counselor before you begin your modelmaking project and tell why they are important.

2. Explain the uses for each of the following types of models: architectural, structural, process, mechanical, and industrial. Do research into the different types of materials that could be used in making these models.

3. With your counselor's advice, select a subject from requirement 4 for your model project (no kits). Prepare the necessary plans to the proper scale, a list of materials to be used, and a list of the required tools. This model should be your own original work. Tell why you selected this subject.

4. Do **one** of the following:

    a. *Architectural model.* Build a model of a house you selected to a scale of ¼"=1'0" (50:1 metric). Discuss with your counselor the materials you intend to use, the amount of detail required, outside treatment (finish, shrubbery, walks, etc.), and color selections. After completing the model, present it to your counselor for approval.

    b. *Structural model.* Build a model showing corner construction of a wood-frame building to a scale of 1½"=1'0" (8:1 metric). All structures shown must be to scale. Cardboard or flat sheet wood stock may be used for sheeting or flooring on the model.

33280
ISBN 0-8395-3280-6
©1993 Boy Scouts of America
2000 Printing of the 1993 Edition

Review with your counselor the problems you encountered in gathering the materials and supporting the structure. Be able to name the parts of the floor and wall frames, such as girder, joist, bridging, subfloor, sole plate, stud, and rafter.

c. *Process model.* Build a model showing the plumbing system in your house. Show hot and cold water supply, all waste returns, and venting to a scale of $\frac{3}{4}$"=1'0" (15:1 metric). Talk to your counselor about how to begin this model, and present the scale and the materials you will use. After completion, present the model to your counselor and be prepared to discuss any problems you had building this model.

d. *Mechanical model.* Build a model of a mechanical device that uses at least two of the six simple machines. After completing the model, present it to your counselor. Be prepared to discuss materials used, the machine's function and use, and any particular difficulty you might have encountered.

e. *Industrial model.* Build a model of an actual passenger-carrying vehicle to a scale of 1"=1'0" or $\frac{1}{2}$"=1'0" (10:1 or 25:1 metric). Take the dimensions of the vehicle and record the important dimensions. Draw the top, front, rear, and sides of the vehicle to scale. From your plans, build a model of the vehicle and finish in a craftsmanlike manner. Discuss with your counselor the most difficult part of completing the model.

5. List at least six occupations in which modelmaking is used and discuss with your counselor some career opportunities in this field.

Contents

Introduction

Engineering models are not new. For centuries, humans have used scale models to communicate thoughts and ideas. The tombs of Egypt, for instance, have yielded many exciting models that depict life in that ancient country so well that we know exactly how the Egyptians harnessed their horses, rigged their ships, armed their warriors, and buried their kings.

Modern engineering modeling started after World War II. Since then it has had a great impact on everyday life. It has helped improve the food we eat. It has helped in the engineering of food processing plants, chemical and plastics plants, power plants, hydraulic structures and systems, oil refineries, and nuclear reactors.

The American Engineering Model Society (AEMS) was formed in 1969. It has grown to include members from many countries around the world. The purpose of AEMS is to get more companies to use engineering models and to find better and more economical ways to build models. As a result, a number of people have selected model-making as a full-time occupation.

This *relief* (a type of sculpture in which parts are raised from the background) models Egyptian farm scenes from thousands of years ago—it is dated at about 2420 B.C. to 2300 B.C. (Photo courtesy the Cleveland Museum of Art, gift of the John Huntington Art and Polytechnic Trust, 30.736.)

Using Hand Tools Safely

These instructions are a basic guide to tool safety. Use tools safely to avoid accidents, reduce injuries, prevent damage to the tools, and improve your model.

There are a lot of dos and don'ts when using hand tools. Try to keep in mind that your hands and eyes are not nearly as tough as a steel hand tool. You might have earned a Totin' Chip for knife and ax safety. The rules of safety when using hand tools on a model are just as important, and the results of poor handling can be just as bad as a split finger due to the improper use of a knife in the field.

A good rule used in most professional model shops is **never work alone.**

General Tips

• Take good care of tools. Keep them clean, oiled, and sharp. Return them to your toolbox when you're finished with them. Don't carry tools around in your pockets.

• Use each tool for what it was made to do. Don't use it for anything else. Pliers aren't hammers. Screwdrivers aren't pry bars.

• Don't use a broken tool. You'll get hurt or you'll mess up your model.

Hand Tools

Hammers and Mallets

• Always use the face of the hammer when striking an object.

• Use only the amount of force needed.

• Never use the claw of the hammer for anything other than removing nails.

• Don't use the handle for anything other than what it was intended for.

Handsaws

- Use a vise to hold the material being sawed.

- On hacksaws and coping saws, adjust blade tension to prevent buckling or breaking. Make sure blades are installed in the correct position.

- Provide sufficient clearance so that, in sawing, the point of the saw will not strike any object.

- Pull and push smoothly and evenly—don't force the saw.

- Don't bend the blade.

- Don't twist the saw in the cut to split off waste material.

- When finished, clean the blade of any foreign material.

- Put the saw in the tool rack when not in use. Don't lay anything on top of the blade.

Screwdrivers

- Use the correct size.

- Keep the handle directly over the screw head.

- Turn with smooth, even strokes.

- Apply steady pressure toward the screw.

- Don't hammer on the handle.

Clamps (C Clamps, Bar Clamps)

- Use the proper size.

- Don't overtighten the clamp.

- During drilling operations, make sure clamps are clear of drilling equipment.

Bench Vises

- Attach the vise to a firm workstand.

- Use the vise to hold materials—don't use your hands.

- Don't overtighten materials in the vise.

- Don't excessively hammer on the jaws of the vise.

- During drilling or cutting operations, make sure you remain clear of the vise body.
- When you are done, close the vise and leave the handle straight up and down.

Hand Files
- Never use a file without a handle.
- Cut in the direction for which the file was intended (mill files—forward stroke, draw files—backward stroke).
- Avoid striking the file teeth or handle with any hard object.
- Avoid laying files on top of each other.
- After use, clean a file with a file card.
- Keep files in a dry place.

Framing Square / Machinist Square
- Don't allow the body to be bent.
- Don't hammer on the body.
- Don't drop the framing square.

Chisels and Gouges
- Wear safety goggles.
- Always securely clamp the material in a bench vise.
- Chip toward the stationary jaw of the vise.
- Use a chisel that's big enough for the job.
- Don't use the chisel or gouge on metal.
- Use the blade, not the point or corner.
- Don't regrind a chisel or gouge—if improperly done, this could ruin it.
- Use only wooden mallets to hammer on chisels and gouges.
- Cover the blades when you are finished.

Twist Drills, Blade Drills, and Countersinks
- Don't regrind or file twist drills. If improperly done, this could damage the drill bit.

- Securely tighten the shank of the twist drill in the chuck.
- Avoid taking heavy cuts through material.
- Avoid running the drill at too high a speed.
- Make sure the twist drill doesn't come in contact with any clamping device.

Router Bits

- Avoid taking heavy cuts through material.
- Cut only materials for which the router bits were intended.

Wrenches (Open-end, Crescent, Socket)

- Use the correct size.
- Pull the wrench toward you, not away from you.
- Avoid using excessive force. Do not use extension bars on wrenches when tightening or loosening bolts.

Hand Drills

- Don't hand-hold the material being drilled.
- Avoid using pliers to tighten twist drills in the chuck.
- Don't force drills into the work.
- Don't hit the handle with hammers or mallets.
- Use sharp bits.
- Use a brush to sweep away chips.

Pliers

- Don't pinch your fingers or hands between the handles.
- When using cutting pliers, don't let the cut piece fly out. Cover it or point it away from you and other people.

Face Shields and Goggles

- Avoid laying face shields or goggles down on their front surface. This scratches the viewing area.
- Clean or wipe off after use.
- Don't overtighten a face shield headband.

Knives

- Don't use a dull or nicked blade.
- Stroke away from the body.
- When finished using the knife, cover the blade and put the knife away.

Scribers

- Use a scriber to mark centerlines or cut lines on plastic material.
- Don't use it as a center punch, pry, or pick.
- When you carry the scriber, hold it by the handle with the point away from you.
- When you're done with it, put it away safely.

Portable Power Tools

- Talk to your counselor and the person you're borrowing the tools from about the safe and proper use of portable power tools.
- Avoid pulling the plug out of the wall by yanking or pulling the cord. Instead, grasp the plug head and pull straight out from the wall socket or extension cord.
- Don't force portable tools to do the work of a heavy-duty tool.
- Don't allow the equipment to be dropped or thrown.
- Don't carry a portable power tool by its cord.
- Arrange the cord so that it won't be in the way of the operation.

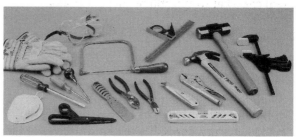

Utility knives
Scissors
Handsaw/coping
  saw
Clamps
Scratch awl
Files
Hammer/mallet
Framing square
Screwdriver
Chisel/gouge

Hand drills and
  drill bits
Pliers

Wrench
Wire cutters
Face shield/goggles

Scale

What does the word "scale" mean? It has lots of meanings. You can weigh things on a scale. A fish has scales. Paint on the side of a building dries up and scales off. You can play a song using a musical scale. You can scale (climb) a wall. You can do something on a grand scale, meaning larger or bigger than normal.

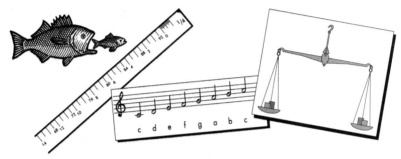

In the engineering and modeling world, *scale* is used to describe *proportion*. Proportion is how the size of one thing compares to another.

If someone says to you, "I'm going to build a model of this telephone to double scale," they mean that the finished model will be twice as big as a normal telephone. Or someone might say, "I'm building a model of this automobile to half scale." Then you would know that the finished model of the car would be only half as big as a real car. That would still be one big model!

A model might be double size (2:1) or half size (1:2), but sometimes that isn't large or small enough. In that case the proportion or scale might be changed to three times as large (3:1) or one-third as big (1:3). As the modeler, you make the decision based on what you want the final size of the model to be.

There are two basic number systems. One is the *foot-and-inch system*. The other is the *metric system,* in which the meter is the basis for all length measures. To keep it simple, we will use only the *foot-and-inch system* for our models.

When we talk about scale from now on, we will talk about the proportions of models or plans as they relate to a one-foot, zero-inch

(1'0") ruler. Let's examine the one-foot ruler as a basis for model scales:

- It has twelve equal parts, each called an inch (you already knew that).
- It can easily be divided into two parts, three parts, four parts, six parts, or twelve parts:

  —Two parts would each be 6" long.

  —Three parts would each be 4" long.

  —Four parts would each be 3" long.

  —Six parts would each be 2" long.

  —Twelve parts would each be 1" long.

In the above example, the 6" part is said to be one-half (1:2) scale or proportion. The 4"-long part is said to be one-third (1:3) scale or proportion.

If in modeling, something is to be built to a scale of 6"=1'0", you would know that the finished model would be one-half (1:2) scale, or one-half the size of the real thing to be built. If something is to be modeled to a scale of 3"=1'0", then you would know that the finished model would be one-fourth (1:4) scale, or one-fourth the size of the real thing to be built.

Most of the time, in modeling buildings, automobiles, or stage sets, for instance, the models are built to an even smaller scale. Suppose a model is to be built to a scale of ¼"=1'0". At that scale, the model will be only ¼ inch long or high for each foot of the "real"

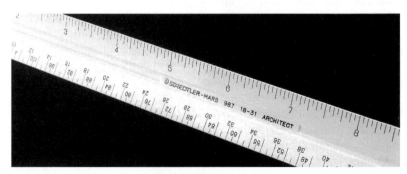

Figure 1. Architect's scale

item. The proportion would be 1:48, or $\frac{1}{48}$ the item's real size. That's because there are forty-eight $\frac{1}{4}$-inch-long pieces in a one-foot ruler.

If you're familiar with Lionel trains, their proportions will give you a good idea of the size of this scale. They were built close to a scale of $\frac{1}{4}$"=1'0". In model railroading, they are called *O gauge* trains.

A wonderful tool helps a modeler build a model to almost any scale. The tool is the architect's rule or scale (figure 1). This triangular ruler displays eleven common scales and a regular one-foot ruler.

Let's see how the $\frac{1}{4}$"=1'0" scale looks on the architect's scale. Some people like to think of each $\frac{1}{4}$" section as a tiny foot-long ruler. Figure 2 shows how the first $\frac{1}{4}$" is divided into twelve small spaces. Each of these little spaces is to be used as a guide for 1" at the $\frac{1}{4}$" scale.

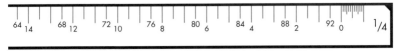

Figure 2. The $\frac{1}{4}$" = 1'0" scale, shown actual size

Following are examples of how to read the $\frac{1}{4}$"=1'0" scale on an architect's scale.

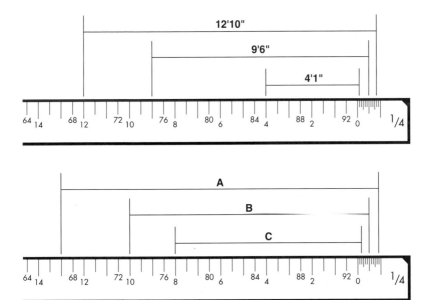

How long is dimension A? _____
How long is dimension B? _____
How long is dimension C? _____
Check your answers with your merit badge counselor.

All the different scales on an architect's scale are read in a similar manner. As an example, look at the ¾"=1'0" scale. How many ¾" pieces are there in a foot-long piece? Count them. If you got sixteen, you are right. The proportion will be 1:16, or 1/16 size. Every foot of the real, finished part would be sixteen times larger than the model. Another way to say it is that each "real" foot vertically or horizontally would be modeled as ¾" long.

You won't need to buy an architect's scale to build your model. The edges of right-hand pages 15 through 35 are printed to duplicate the eleven scales on the architect's scale. When you choose a scale to build your model, simply cut the edge of the page off and glue it to a piece of cardboard or wood. Glue it so that the marks line up with the edge of the cardboard. See figure 3.

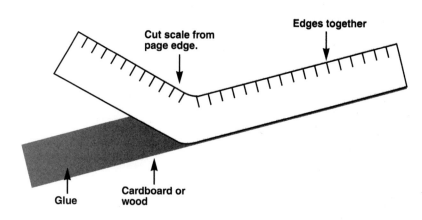

Figure 3. Glue scale from edge of page to cardboard or wood backer.

Materials and Finishes

Modelmakers are experts on materials and finishes. They use all sorts of things for making models, some of which the average person might not even consider. A trip to a local, well-equipped model supply store will give you many ideas to use on your model for this merit badge.

The choice of materials is vast. This section offers ideas about where you can find modeling materials. Of course, anyone can go out and buy scale model parts. The trick is to use things found around the house to come up with a good model.

Glue and Paint

For some types of models, you will have to buy some supplies in a store. Glue and paint are examples of these. Be sure to use glue and paint that will not damage the materials you choose. Some glues and paints contain solvents that can eat away your model. Check with the seller of the product to see if it will hurt your materials. Another test is to try a little on a scrap piece and watch the results.

Wood and Polystyrene Foam

Probably the material most used for models is wood. Soft woods such as balsa, pine, or basswood are easily worked. Thin sheets of wood such as those from orange crates and other packing boxes are ideal model material. Wood can be nailed or glued with model airplane cement, and it sands well for a nice finish. Some models are made from larger blocks of wood and are carved or sawed to the shape desired.

Large blocks of dense polystyrene foam (commonly known by the trade name Styrofoam) can also be used.

Cardboard

Probably the second most-used material in model building is cardboard. You can get cardboard from many places. The backs of writing tablets are a good source. Old shoeboxes or gift boxes also are excellent. Manila file folders, such as those used in an office, are a fine source of thin cardboard.

Adhesive tape can be used on cardboard. White glue and rubber cement work better and are more permanent.

If you have a little money and want to use a material that many architects build models with, go to an art supply store and get a sheet or two of illustration board. Known to artists and designers by the trade name Crescent board, this is a heavy, laminated paper board that has a smooth surface and can be cut with a utility knife. Be careful when using the knife. (See the chapter titled "Using Hand Tools Safely.")

Materials and Uses

The following list will help you get started collecting materials for your modelmaking project. Remember, choose your project first. Talk it over with your counselor and get his or her ideas. A good Scout uses his resources.

Material	Use on Model
Tongue depressors, Popsicle sticks	Wood or metal beams, house siding, links in a breadboard or 3-D mechanical model
Straws, uncooked spaghetti, dowel sticks, coat hanger wire, pencils, matchsticks	Pipes and columns, axles, push rods, dowels, fenceposts, telephone poles
Styrofoam meat tray (flat bottom)	House wall sections, inside walls; any flat surface in a house (even stairs)

Straight pins, thumbtacks	Stuck in straws to show valve locations on pipes; used to hold Styrofoam in place while gluing; used in breadboard models as pivot points
Sandpaper (different colors)	House roofs, blacktop driveways, any textured surface; glued on to make a surface rough for friction drives
Twigs from shrubbery with many branches	Trees
Cotton, lichens, sponges	Painted as shrubs and tree foliage draped over twigs
Plaster of paris	Used to mold irregular forms
Soup or vegetable cans, rolled oats boxes	Tanks on a process model, rollers, large pipes
Rubber bands	Belt or chain drives
Cloth or canvas	Any irregular surface covering
Clear bread wrapping, plastic wrap	Window glass
Sewing thread	Cables, telephone wires
Sawdust	Sprinkled over wet rubber cement on a surface to make grass; paint it green

Selection

Naturally, you will come up with many more materials to use in your model. Remember when you select a material to perform a certain function in a model that it must be strong enough to hold up.

Using a piece of thin cardboard or Styrofoam as a push rod in an engine model wouldn't work. The cardboard would buckle and the Styrofoam might crunch. You would need something stronger, like wood or metal. And the thickness of the material must be considered. For instance, if you used coat hanger wire for a long push rod it would probably bend. If you used it for a short one, it might work fine.

Craftsmanship

One final word about materials: consider craftsmanship when you assemble your model. A model made of six or seven different materials, even though each material is finished well, can look junky. When you choose your materials, keep this in mind. Try to choose finishes such as paint or varnish that can be used on several different parts of your model, preferably all of them.

In business and industry, models are often used to test how the real product will work, to help sell an idea, or to explain a mechanism or process to a client. So, good craftsmanship is important.

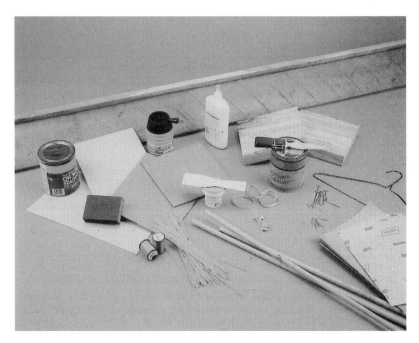

Types of Models

Many different types of models can be constructed to serve different purposes. Hobbyists build model aircraft, cars, trains, boats, houses, furniture, and other items in miniature simply because it's fun to make them.

Other models have special uses in business and industry. Automobile manufacturers, for instance, often use models to test the *aerodynamic* design or wind resistance of vehicles. Filmmakers use models to achieve breathtaking special effects in movies. Engineers use models in designing dams and flood-control structures. Furniture designers use models to help make chairs, desks, bedsteads, and tables more attractive and more comfortable to use. Other uses for professional-quality models are listed in the section of this pamphlet that discusses modelmaking as a career.

An engineering model, such as this model of a dam spillway, can be used to test how well a design works before actual construction begins. (Model courtesy Freese and Nichols, Inc., Consulting Engineers.)

For requirement 4, you are to build *one* of the following types of models used in business and industry:

- *architectural*—a model of a house
- *structural*—a model showing corner construction of a wood-frame building
- *process*—a model of the plumbing system in a house
- *mechanical*—a model of a mechanism that does some kind of work
- *industrial*—a model of a passenger-carrying vehicle

Before choosing which to build, read the following sections to find out more about each type. Though only one model is required for this merit badge, you may build more than one.

Architectural Models

Architecture is the art of designing buildings. Architects and engineers often use models to see how the buildings they design will look, in miniature, before construction begins on the full-scale structure. Models are important design aids because even the most carefully rendered drawings and blueprints will not include all of the detail that can be shown in a model. Drawings are flat, or two-dimensional, while a model shows a structure in three dimensions.

You don't have to be an architect or an engineer to design and build model houses and other buildings. For requirement 4, you can make a model of the house in which you live now, or one you would like to live in someday. Your model could be of a log cabin, a frontier fort, a castle, a train station, or some famous structure like the White House or the Taj Mahal. Or you might want to design something out of this world—a fantastic home of the future, perhaps, or living quarters inside an orbiting space station.

Plans and Materials

To begin, draw a *floor plan* of the house you are going to model. If you are making a model of an existing building, take careful measurements of the building and draw a floor plan based on your measurements. As a guide, use the sample floor plan shown. Or you can base your design on a floor plan printed in a book or magazine. Many pre-drawn plans are available. Check your local library or a do-it-yourself type of building supply store for ideas.

Note that the sample plan is drawn to a scale of ⅛"=1'0". Thus the outside dimensions of the house, 32' by 56', are drawn on the plan as 4" by 7". (The height of the house is not shown, but for a typical one-story house you can assume a standard height of 8' from the top of the foundation to the eaves of the roof, plus another 4' from the eaves to the peak of the roof.) Requirement 4 specifies that the model be built to a scale of ¼"=1'0". This means that a model based

Figure 4. Floor plan and elevation

on the sample floor plan would measure 8" by 14", and 3" high from foundation to roof peak.

When your floor plan is done, use its dimensions in measuring and marking the building materials for your model. You may use wood or cardboard. Cardboard is simple to work with, inexpensive, easy to get, and durable if treated with reasonable care. Wood is strong and attractive, but more difficult to work. If you choose wood, consider purchasing some lengths of *lattice wood* from a lumberyard. Lattice wood is a ¼"-thick wood that comes in long strips. It can be bought in various widths from about ¾" to 3" wide. An 8' strip of lattice wood 1½" wide costs very little and can provide a good part of the material required for a fair-sized house model.

Feel free to experiment with creative types of construction and out-of-the-ordinary styles. Some hobbyists build highly elaborate model houses using unusual building materials including plastic, foil, and polystyrene foam. Use your imagination. For example, the round cardboard tubes on which aluminum foil, waxed paper, and toilet paper are wrapped can be used to create castle towers, or round rooms in a modernistic office building, or transfer tunnels in a space station.

21

Steps in Assembly

The drawings that follow illustrate the basic steps in making a model of a simple building.

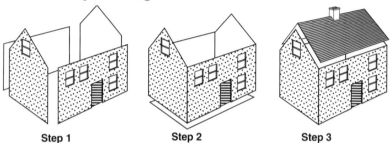

Step 1   Step 2   Step 3

Figure 5. Basic steps in assembling a house model

1. Measure and cut out the exterior walls. Draw and cut out the window and door openings. (It's easy to cut out door and window openings at this stage, while the walls can be laid flat on a work surface; it's difficult to make neat openings after the walls are fastened together.)

2. Apply glue to the edges and assemble the walls. Measure and cut out a base and glue it into position. (If you plan to later add a porch, walkway, shrubbery, trees, or other outside treatments, extend the base far enough beyond the walls of the house to allow room for the additions.)

3. Make a peaked roof from one large piece of cardboard, scored and folded at the peak. To *score* cardboard, make a shallow groove by running a dull knife blade along the line where the fold is to be. A butter knife works well. Use a ruler as a guide so that the score, and the fold, will be straight. Make the score on the inside of the fold—in this case, on the underside of the roof. If you want to be able to remove the roof to look inside the model or to add interior walls later, don't glue it down. Cut the roof so that it hangs over slightly on the ends and sides; the overhanging edge is called the *eave.*

To make this basic house model more realistic and attractive, add some architectural details:

• Cut and fold cardboard to form a front porch and steps, or make them from blocks of wood.

- Use thin strips of wood or cardboard to add shutters, window frames, and door frames.

- Use clear plastic, plastic wrap, or transparent adhesive tape for window panes. Glue colored tissue paper or fabric behind windows for curtains.

- Attach an extra room or shed simply by adding a box to the main structure.

- To add a chimney, first fashion a small box. Then cut a V-shaped notch from the bottom of opposite sides of the box to fit the slope of the roof.

- Add interest to a large, unbroken expanse of roof by attaching dormer windows as shown in the drawings.

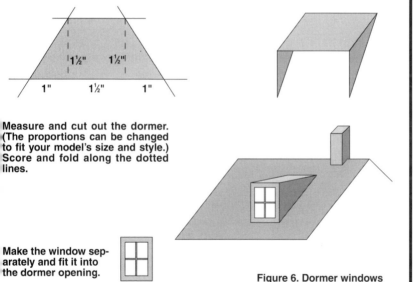

1½" **1½"**

1" **1¼"** **1"**

Measure and cut out the dormer. (The proportions can be changed to fit your model's size and style.) Score and fold along the dotted lines.

Make the window separately and fit it into the dormer opening.

Figure 6. Dormer windows

Outside Treatments

Finish your architectural model with an interesting surface texture or treatment. The following will give you some ideas for wall and roof finishes.

Walls

- Paint or stain. Paint shutters and door and window trims a contrasting color.

- Draw light pencil lines to suggest wood siding.

- Scribe shallow, parallel grooves with a pointed tool to suggest tongue-and-groove siding.

- Glue on strips of thin cardboard or balsa wood to resemble clapboard siding.

- Apply a sand texture to resemble concrete. To create this effect, paint a heavy layer of glue onto the walls. (Do this before the walls are glued together so that you can lay the walls flat on your work surface.) Sprinkle on a handful of fine sand, such as that used in aquariums. Let the glue harden, then shake off the excess sand. The same method can be used with materials such as sawdust and ashes to create unusual surface textures and finishes.

- Spackle walls to resemble stucco. Brush a little water over each unattached cardboard wall section and apply an even layer of white glue. Sprinkle generously with powdered Spackle (a brand of quick-drying, plasterlike material for patching plasterwork). Tap off the excess powder. Lay the wall facedown on a clean piece of cardboard and rub the back to make the Spackled surface smooth. Turn the wall faceup and let the glue set. To color the walls like real stucco, use spirit-based wood stain, shellac, or paint. When the paint is dry, back each wall with a piece of thick cardboard for extra support.

- Apply individual cardboard "bricks." Cut small rectangles from gray or colored cardboard and glue them onto the walls. To keep the brick courses even, draw guidelines or glue graph paper onto the walls. Spread enough white glue over a section of wall to lay about three square inches of bricks at a time. Position each brick with the point of a knife. (As with sand and stucco texturing, "bricking" a house model should be done before the walls are glued together so that you can work with the walls laid out flat.) To get a red-brick look, paint the walls with a wash of mahogany wood stain. Use shellac to imitate yellow bricks.

Roof Surfaces

- Lay cardboard tiles. Cut individual roof tiles from very thin cardboard. Mark guidelines on the roof to help you keep the rows even as you glue on each tile, using the point of a knife to accurately position each one. For the most realistic effect, overlap and stagger each row of tiles. Cap the peak of the roof with ridge tiles. To make ridge tiles, cut out a narrow strip of thin cardboard. Score it down the middle, then cut the strip into individual tiles. Fold each tile in half along the score line and glue it onto the roof ridge. Color the roof with a wash of mahogany wood stain. Or, to resemble roofing slates, color with gray, blue, and white washes.

- Use masking tape to resemble wooden shingles. Cut rectangles from strips of paper masking tape and apply the paper shingles in the same way as cardboard tiles. Use wood stain to color the roof and to dull the shine of the masking tape.

- Glue on straw or reeds to model a traditional English thatched roof.

- Apply aluminum foil to suggest a metal roof.

Structural Models

An architectural model shows what a building will look like, but it doesn't necessarily show how the building will be constructed. The walls and roof in an architectural model might be little more than flat sheets of cardboard or wood. In a structural model, however, details of construction are shown. The individual pieces that make up floor, wall, and roof structures are reproduced in miniature.

One option for requirement 4 is to build a model showing corner construction of a wood-frame building. If you've never had the chance to help build a house or to watch one being built, then you might not know much about the techniques of wood-frame construction. The following outlines the basic steps in framing the floor, walls, and roof supports of a house. You'll need to understand these basic elements, and the terms used to name them, before you can build an accurate model showing corner construction.

Wood-Frame Construction

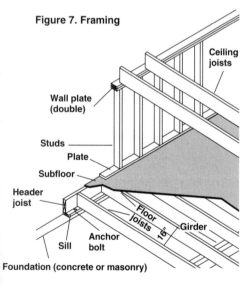

Figure 7. Framing

Ceiling joists

Wall plate (double)

Studs

Plate

Subfloor

Header joist

Floor joists 16"

Girder

Sill

Anchor bolt

Foundation (concrete or masonry)

In wood-frame construction over concrete or masonry block foundation walls, the first wooden member of the structure is the *sill.* Sills (also called plates or sole plates) are placed flat (horizontally) on top of the concrete foundation walls all around the structure and are secured to the foundation with anchor bolts. The material usually used for sills is 2" by 6" lumber (known to builders as 2×6s, written without the inch marks). The lumber should be long enough, if possible, to run the full length of the walls; otherwise it can be butted end to end. In some areas of the country, building codes require a 4"-thick sill, which is achieved simply by stacking a second 2 × 6 on top of the first. It's also common practice to double up 2 × 6s to create a 4" sill when building in areas of heavy winds.

Floor joists are horizontal members of the structure, placed on edge, that span the foundation walls. Joists run parallel to each other and are evenly spaced between the sills. In house building, the spacing of joists is fairly standard at 16" from the center of one joist to the center of the next, but the spacing can vary greatly depending on the load the joists will be carrying. Houses with plastered walls and ceilings and tile roofs are much heavier than houses built with plywood walls, acoustical ceilings, and shingles. For your purposes in designing a structural model, you may assume that the joists are 2 × 6s spaced 16" apart, with a span of 12'.

Because the span is only 12'—not far enough to reach the entire distance between the foundation walls—the joists will need supports between the sills. The supports are called beams or *girders*. The ends of the girders rest on the foundation walls in special pockets provided for them, and the girders are themselves supported between the foundation walls on posts. Girders can be solid blocks of timber. More commonly, they are built up from two or more layers of 2"-thick lumber. For your purposes in modelmaking, assume that the girders are 4 × 6s (that is, they are built up from two layers of 2 × 6 lumber) and are spaced 6' apart.

Floor joists that are too short to run the entire length of the structure, and so must be pieced together, are overlapped where they cross the girder. Solid *bridging* can be nailed between them for support, or installed at other points between joists to keep them fixed and straight. A common system of bridging uses pieces of 1 × 3 or 1 × 4 lumber set between joists as shown in figure 8. The bridging should be in a straight line, at a spacing of 8' or midway

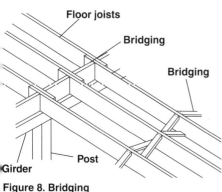

Floor joists

Bridging

Bridging

Girder

Post

Figure 8. Bridging

27

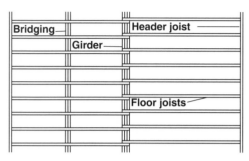

Figure 9. Floor frame

between the foundation wall and the girder (figure 9).

Floor joists are boxed in by *headers* that run across the ends of the joists. The headers are attached to the sills.

On top of the floor frame formed by the joists and headers, common 1" boards or ⅝" plywood sheets are placed to form the *subfloor.* The subfloor adds rigidity to the structure and acts as a base for the final, finished floor.

Wall frames are installed next. They support upper structures like ceilings and roofs and act as bases on which the builder can fasten exterior and interior wall coverings. Inside the wall frames between the coverings, there is room for other house essentials such as electrical wiring, telephone cables, water and gas pipes, heating ducts, and insulation.

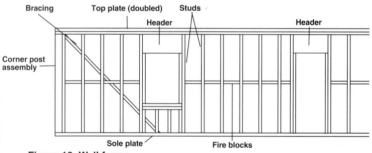

Figure 10. Wall frame

The lowermost member of the wall frame is the *sole plate,* a long piece of 2×4 lumber placed flat and nailed along the edge of the subflooring. *Studs* are the upright or vertical members of the wall frame. Studs usually are 2×4s, but 2×6s may be used if a thicker wall is desired. (If 2×6s are used, the sole plate also will be of 2×6 lumber.) Studs are nailed to the plate. Usually they are spaced either 16" or 24" apart.

Assemblies of 2×4 (or 2×6) lumber called *posts* are used at the corners of wall frames. A basic post design uses two studs and three spacers nailed together to form a solid unit. When the post is for a corner, a third stud is added as shown in figure 11.

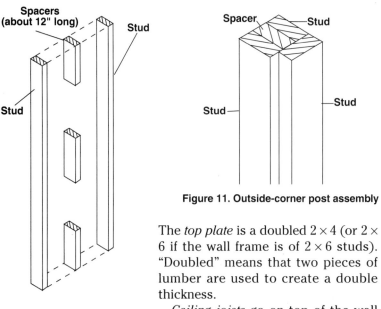

Figure 11. Outside-corner post assembly

The *top plate* is a doubled 2×4 (or 2×6 if the wall frame is of 2×6 studs). "Doubled" means that two pieces of lumber are used to create a double thickness.

Ceiling joists go on top of the wall frames. Like floor joists, they are horizontal members of the structure placed on edge; they run parallel to each other and are evenly spaced, usually 16" apart. Unlike floor joists, they have no headers around the edges. Ceiling joists act as ties between opposite walls and support the ceiling.

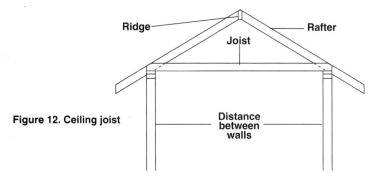

Figure 12. Ceiling joist

Rafters are sloping timbers that support the roof. Rafters typically are spaced 16" to 24" apart.

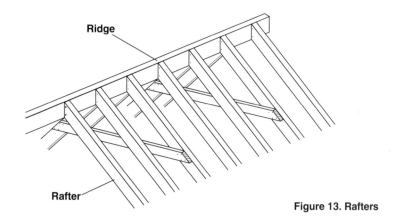

Figure 13. Rafters

Building to Scale

The structural model for requirement 4 is to be built to a scale of $1\frac{1}{2}$"=1'0". At this scale, 2×6 lumber would be represented by strips of wood $\frac{1}{4}$" thick by $\frac{3}{4}$" wide. To model a 2×4, use a strip $\frac{1}{4}$" thick by $\frac{1}{2}$" wide.

Before beginning to build your model, prepare a supply of miniature 2×4s and 2×6s. Also prepare the other necessary building materials to the same scale—you might need small pieces to use for bridging, and cardboard or flat sheet wood stock for flooring. Although nails or screws would be used to hold the various parts together in full-scale construction, you may use glue in making your model.

Study the illustrations carefully to see how the subfloor, wall, and roof structures in a wood-frame building work together to support the building. In constructing your model, work slowly and let the framework dry between steps. If you rush the project, you could end up with a messy pile of wooden sticks instead of the strongly built, accurately scaled, and professionally constructed model that is your goal.

Process Models

Phenol production plant

A process model is used to show an idea, in three dimensions, for locating equipment and pipes for the making of a product. Process models are built by engineers to show on a small scale what a manufacturing plant will look like when constructed. A model of such a plant can be easily understood by its viewer because it is almost like looking at the real thing, except it is much smaller.

Models are used in designing process plants, such as for drug companies making vitamin pills, aspirin, and other medicines; companies processing and packaging foods and beverages; and chemical companies that make inks, dyes, and paints. These are just a few examples of where models are used.

Types of Process Models

There are two types of process models: *planning models* and the *final construction models* from which construction workers actually build the full-size plant.

A planning model is simple. Usually it is made of inexpensive materials and is built quickly. It is used to convey an idea for the general location of pipes and equipment. You could use wood, cardboard, string, blocks, foam, or any material that is handy. The idea is to show the concept, not the details, so a preliminary planning model doesn't include a lot of detail. Equipment is shown as plain blocks and usually only large groups of pipe are shown. The main purpose of a planning model is to see if pipes and equipment will fit into the spaces available.

A final construction model is much more complex, accurate, and expensive. It shows far more detail than the planning model. Equipment is modeled in exact detail and with such accuracy that you can see what each item is. Instead of showing pipes as blocks of materials, each pipe is shown individually and cemented into place.

Definition of Terms

Before you continue, you need to know some terms used in process modeling. You will use some of these in building your model:

Elbow. A pipe fitting used to change the direction of a pipe.

Fire protection. Fireplugs, hoses, and sprinklers used to put out fires.

HVAC. Heating, ventilating, and air-conditioning.

Instrumentation. Automatic devices used to operate valves, take readings, show temperatures, etc.

Pipe. Hollow tubing used to convey a liquid, a gas, or a product from one place to another.

Pump. Equipment used to force a product through a pipeline.

Structure. The building or framework used to enclose the process.

Tank. Tub used to store a liquid, a gas, or a product.

Tee. A pipe fitting used to branch off of a pipe to go in another direction.

Valve. A device that controls the flow of a product, liquid, or gas through a pipe, like a faucet in a bathroom.

Advantages of Models

Building a model before beginning actual construction has many advantages. During the design stage, a model allows you to see interferences easily. For example, you can spot places where two different things will try to take up the same space: a piece of equipment that sticks out into an aisle or hits a tank, for instance.

Because a three-dimensional model shows equipment in length, width, and height, layouts can be judged better. Engineers can decide the best locations for welding, for pipe and equipment supports, for water hose stations, for lights, and for items such as valves. Safety items such as safety showers (where operators accidentally splashed with acid can be drenched with water) are easily placed on a model.

One of the most important advantages of a process model is that the model serves as the main place where architects, piping engineers, and machine designers can gather and work out their problems together. All of the engineers can coordinate their work through the use of the model. When the process model is complete, it is used not only for construction purposes, but also, in many cases, to train the workers who will operate the final plant after it is constructed.

What Process Models Show

You have learned what a process model is, who uses process models, and the advantages of building one. Now consider in more detail what is shown on a process model.

Building Structure

After the size (scale or proportion) and shape of the model has been decided, the modeler makes the structure of the building to enclose the plant. (However, some models are of outside equipment and piping and would not be enclosed in a structure.) The building structure can be made of wood, plastic, cardboard, or any material available that will do the job. Beams and columns are usually shown to the largest outside dimensions or, to be more realistic, sometimes the actual shape is shown.

The modelmaker might want to show the walls in some material only partially. Modelmakers call this "dodging in" a wall. Partial sections are used because the modelmaker wishes to leave access to actually work on the model. If the walls are put in completely, no one could get hands or tools in to work on the model.

Equipment Layout

Equipment should be placed in the model in its exact location, taking care to ensure that it is accurately positioned and that there is adequate space left in which to get around the equipment. A good rule is to allow a 36" (3') minimum access around each piece of equipment. (Remember, at a scale of $\frac{3}{4}$"=1'0", $\frac{3}{4}$" $\times$ 3 = $\frac{9}{4}$" = $2\frac{1}{4}$". That is, the modelmaker would need to leave a space of $2\frac{1}{4}$" around each piece of equipment in the model to represent the 36" minimum access required in the actual plant.)

Equipment can be modeled to any degree of detail desired. It can be made of wood, cardboard or plastic boxes, cardboard tubes, or any material that is easily adapted to the shape needed. The section titled "Materials and Finishes" lists other materials useful in building process models.

Piping

Piping takes careful thought and planning before installation. When many pipelines are to be shown, the modelmaker must consider the order they are in, the size of the pipes, how they will be supported, and how a worker would reach any valves that might be in the pipes. In positioning pipes, designers and engineers must try to use only the minimum number of fittings required to get from one point to another. Unnecessary fittings increase the cost of materials and increase labor costs to install them.

Other things to consider are head clearances and sloped lines. Sloped pipelines are those that must drain by gravity. In basements you will see sink and toilet drainpipes that are sloped.

Heating and Ventilating

Another important part of a manufacturing plant that can be shown on a model is the heating and ventilating equipment and ductwork. Heating and ventilating equipment does just that: it heats the building, air-conditions the building, and provides good ventilation. Ductwork is the "pipeline" through which warm or cold air travels. Equipment and ductwork must be put in so that pipes, electrical wires, and other equipment do not go through or interfere with the ducts.

Instrumentation and Electrical Conduits

Most equipment needs electricity to operate. Much of the equipment used in manufacturing plants is made to operate by electrical signals from different types of instruments. These can include automatic valves, switches, transmitters, and recording devices. Therefore, it is important that electrical conduits and instruments are properly installed.

Building a Process Model

Now that you know what kinds of things can be shown on a big industrial process model, you're ready to build a similar, though simpler, model of your own. One kind of process almost everyone is familiar with is the water system in a house. Water is piped into a house; some of it is left cold and some is heated, and then the water is distributed throughout the house.

Figure 14 is a flow diagram of a simple water system you can use as a guide in building a model of the plumbing system in your home. The plumbing in your house might have more attachments on the pipelines than shown in the diagram. Look for them all. If you have a question about what you see, ask your counselor. If you have radiators in your home, ask an adult to explain to you how they work.

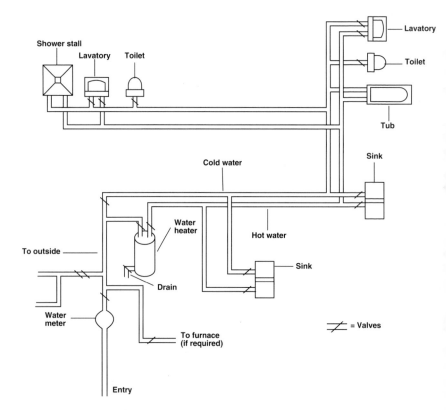

Figure 14. Diagram of basic plumbing system

Mechanical Models

Models are an easy-to-understand means of presenting and communicating ideas. As such, they are affecting many career areas. Machine designers use models to find answers to complex machine questions. Tool and die designers use them to determine the proper tooling and dies to use on machine tools. Many engineering firms use models. These include research and development, automotive, and mechanical models.

A mechanical model is no different from other models, in that it is used to help people understand an idea. Mechanical models usually are made up of two or more of the six simple machines you learned about in science class: wheel and axle, lever, wedge, inclined plane, screw, and pulley (see figure 15). When model designers and engineers think about a mechanical model or mechanism, they know it is a combination of these simple machines put together to do some kind of work.

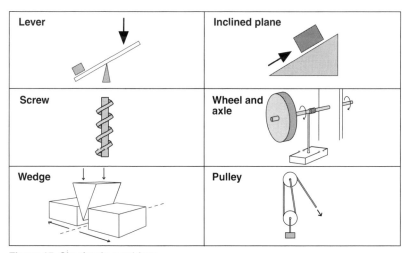

Figure 15. Six simple machines

Basic Mechanisms

In a mechanical model there are at least two of the simple machines mentioned above, used together. One of the parts will be stationary, or held in one place. That part is called a *driver*. The other part moves and is called a *follower*. Sometimes the second part will move back and forth along a straight line. It could move back and forth along a curved line or a circular path. It could move only in part of a circle, called an *arc*.

The illustrations show some examples of mechanical models.

Wheel and Axle

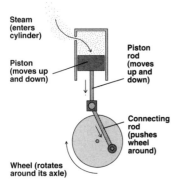

Figure 16 shows an example of a mechanism that changes an up-and-down movement into a circular motion. Steam goes into the cylinder and pushes on the piston and piston rod, which can only move up and down. The piston rod is attached to a connecting rod, which pushes the wheel around on its axle as the piston moves up and down. Most steam engines and gasoline engines work on this principle.

Figure 16. The piston's up-and-down movement is changed into circular motion.

Four-Bar Linkage

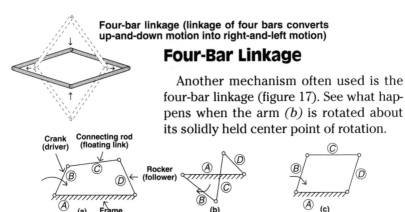

Another mechanism often used is the four-bar linkage (figure 17). See what happens when the arm *(b)* is rotated about its solidly held center point of rotation.

Figure 17. Four-bar mechanisms: (a) open, (b) crossed, (c) parallel

Some common tools that use mechanisms are shown in figure 18. The locking plier is an example of four-bar linkage with the fixed link made adjustable by turning the end screw.

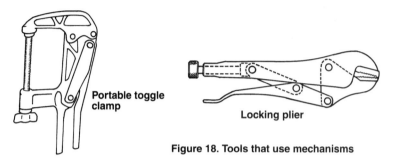

Portable toggle clamp

Locking plier

Figure 18. Tools that use mechanisms

Straight-Line Mechanisms

A straight-line mechanism causes a point to travel in a straight or nearly straight line, without being guided by a plane surface. Such mechanisms were important in the early days of machinery before machine tools were invented to make smooth plane surfaces. James Watt, a Scottish inventor and mechanical engineer, had a great need for a mechanism that would guide the joint between the piston rod and the drive beam along a straight line in his steam engine.

Figure 19. Straight-line mechanisms

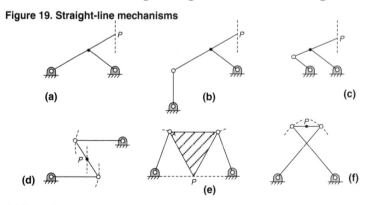

(a) Scott-Russell
(b) and (c) variations of Scott-Russell
(d) Watt's
(e) Robert's
(f) Tchebycheff's

P=point traveling in straight line
= fixed pivot

39

Cams

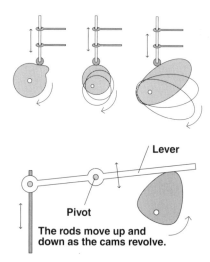

The rods move up and down as the cams revolve.

Cam mechanisms provide a simple means of getting unusual or irregular motions that would be difficult, if not impossible, to obtain with other types of mechanizing. The *cam* is any guiding surface and the *follower* usually is a little wheel that is either lifted or guided by the cam surface. Cams are the heart of such automatic devices as automatic machine tools and record changers, and they are found in all internal combustion engines.

Figure 20. Examples of cams. Cams with irregular or unusual shapes can be used to achieve a desired motion. In other cases a simple round or oval wheel mounted so that it revolves off-center will guide the follower in the desired motion.

Gears

Gears are toothed wheels used to transmit a motion accurately in the form of a circular motion from one part to another. Before gears were invented, people used friction rollers for this purpose. But the

One gear turns in one direction, the other gear in the opposite direction.

The large gear on the left will turn more slowly than the small gear on the right.

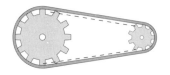

A sprocket gear's teeth are designed to work with a chain. A bicycle has sprocket gears.

Figure 21. Gears

40

two rollers often slipped when a load was applied to them—the speed of the two rollers could not be kept the same when they were supposed to be transmitting power. The rollers were said to be "slipping." With gears the two rollers have teeth and are locked together so that they can't slip.

To make two gears rotate without slipping but without touching, the modelmaker or engineer uses a chain to connect the two gears. A bicycle chain is a perfect example of this arrangement. When referring to a chain drive, the designer or engineer calls the gears *sprockets* instead of gears. Gears and chain drives are good parts to use when you build your mechanical model.

Building a Mechanical Model

Models of mechanisms are used in the first stages of design to ensure that the design will do what it is supposed to do. *Breadboard* (flat) models are among the easiest types to make. They can be cut out of cardboard, poster board, or paper. The pieces of cardboard or paper can be fastened to a backer board with thumbtacks and can be made to move or remain stationary. Because the materials used are rather flimsy, this type of model has limited usefulness.

Prototype models can be made of many materials including wood, plastic, and metal. They usually are three-dimensional, in contrast to breadboard models, which usually are two-dimensional. Prototype models can be made full-size or to a different scale. Design information gained from such models can be of real value.

"Sales models" often are made to promote the sale of a new item. Sometimes they are referred to as "suitcase models" because they can be carried from one place to another in a suitcase. They can be three-dimensional or two-dimensional models and are made from a variety of materials similar to those previously mentioned.

When choosing a mechanical model to build, you might consider making a model of a two-wheel bicycle chain drive, a new kind of lock mechanism, or a big model of the squirting mechanism on a bottle of window cleaner (maybe you could even make it squirt water). Use your imagination.

Discuss your choice with your counselor before you start.

SIDE VIEW

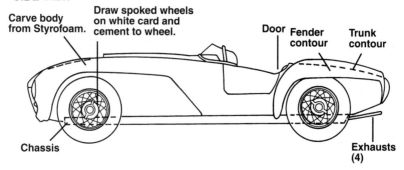

Carve body from Styrofoam.

Draw spoked wheels on white card and cement to wheel.

Door

Fender contour

Trunk contour

Chassis

Exhausts (4)

FRONT VIEW

Air scoop

Engine hatch

Headlight

Thin wire grille

Chassis

Wheels

REAR VIEW

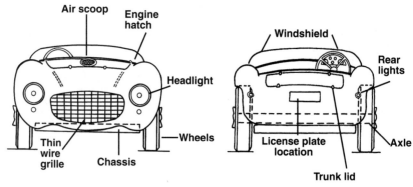

Windshield

Rear lights

License plate location

Trunk lid

Axle

TOP VIEW

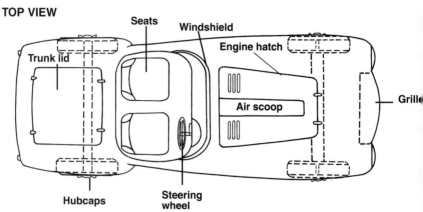

Seats

Windshield

Engine hatch

Trunk lid

Air scoop

Grille

Hubcaps

Steering wheel

42

Industrial Models

Almost all products—cars, appliances, toys, furniture—begin as models. As you have learned, models are used to see how something works or looks before it is manufactured or built. These first models are prototypes.

You may complete requirement 4 by building an industrial model. The example is a car. Other industrial models also are acceptable, with the approval of your counselor.

Plans, Materials, and Tools

Several materials, including wood, clay, plastic, and cardboard, are suitable for building industrial models. Styrofoam is suggested for a car. It is inexpensive, easy to work, and can be found at most hobby and florist shops. If you use Styrofoam, you also will need a water-soluble white glue (not plastic model cement), spackling paste (commonly used for patching wall cracks), a sharp knife, sandpaper, and paint. To make a drawing, you will need a pencil, paper, and a ruler.

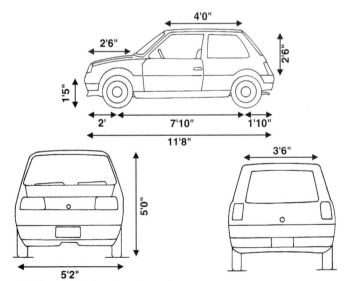

Figure 22. Car—side, front, and rear views

Before you begin drawing, you must first select a design. It can be a copy of an existing car or your own creation. If it's a copy, be sure it's a car that will be available for reference as you build your model. If the design is your own, keep it simple. Most things are easier to draw than they are to build.

Start your drawing with a side view to a scale of 1"=1'0". Your drawing should include overall dimensions and important reference points. Working from front to back, these might include the distance from the ground to the bumper, the height of the grille, the length of the hood, the distance from the ground to the roof, and so on. The drawing also should include front and rear views as shown in the example.

When you have completed your drawing, show it to your counselor. Discuss any questions and review the next steps. With your counselor's approval, you are ready to start the model.

Making the Model

Transfer the outline of the side view from your drawing to the Styrofoam. This is best done by making a paper pattern and tracing around it. If the Styrofoam is 1" thick, you will need five or six layers, depending on the overall width of the car. Each layer will be identical except for wheel openings in the outside layers.

When you have cut out all of the layers, glue them together with common white glue and let them dry for several hours. *Note:* Do not use plastic model cement on Styrofoam. The foam will melt and the layers will not bond.

When the glue has dried, the block can be carved. This step is intended to give the model its basic form, not its detail. An ordinary kitchen knife and a hacksaw blade are perfect tools for carving Styrofoam.

After you have finished carving the shape, spread a layer of spackling paste over the foam. It will take several hours for the paste to dry, so set the model aside until the next day.

When the paste is thoroughly dry, lightly sand the model with fine sandpaper. Then use a pointed tool and a fine file or piece of sandpaper to shape the details of the model. Scribe the outlines of window frames and windows, doors, hood, trunk lid, radiator grille, headlights, taillights, etc.

Make wheels and tires from disks of wood. Glue the disks into the wheel openings. Or for a more realistic effect, mount the wheels on axles of coat hanger wire or a similar material so that the car will roll.

Paint your model. When the base coats are completely dry, you can add details such as pin-striping and whitewall tires. Use a fine-bristled, pointed brush for painting pinstripes, body side molding, numbers on the sides and hood of a race car, and other delicate paintwork.

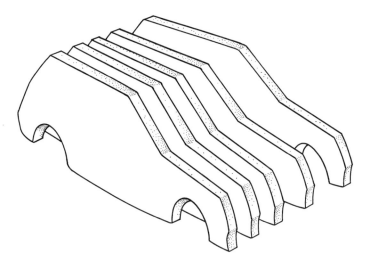

Figure 23. Transfer the outline of the side view to 1"-thick Styrofoam. Cut out five or six layers, depending on the overall width of the car. Each layer will be identical except for wheel openings in the outside layers. Glue the layers together.

Make wheels from disks of wood. Mount them on axles of coat hanger wire or a similar material inserted through the wheel openings.

Modelmaking As a Career

Industrial modeling is a relatively new career area. It has become popular within the past thirty years. A few colleges and vocational training schools in the United States offer associate degree programs in modeling technology (also called modelbuilding, model construction, or industrial modelmaking).*

Computer modeling also is a relatively new and growing career field. Computers are making it possible to "build" and display intricate models on-screen; though such models have no physical form, they can be studied and manipulated on computer monitors much as scale models in three dimensions. In the future, computer models might replace scale models for some design purposes, but industry will continue to need and use a variety of detailed, 3-D models.

Industry's need for trained technicians is growing yearly. Industrial modeling is not only profitable, but also enjoyable for those who pursue this occupation. Consider the following options.

Business Area	How Models Are Used
Automobile industry	Sales, wind resistance testing, human environmental models, safety design
Toy industry	Development and sales models
Chemical and petroleum industries	Process piping models, offshore drilling rigs, ship design, dry materials handling

---

*At the time this pamphlet was written, the schools that offered training in industrial modelmaking were Community College of Allegheny County—South Campus, West Mifflin, Pennsylvania; Genesee Community College, Batavia, New York; Macomb County Community College—South Campus, Warren, Michigan; Mission College, Santa Clara, California; and Traviss Vocational Technical Center, Lakeland, Florida. Your merit badge counselor, teacher, or school counselor can help you find information about training opportunities near your home.

Office equipment	Concept models, sales, touch (texture) and form models, human factors engineering
Movies and theaters	Stage sets, robots, makeup
Machine tools	Studies of movements, forces; internal strain models
Building and construction (architectural/structural)	Buildings and houses, office layouts, structural steel models, color models, site study models (cities, urban planning, site reconstruction, and historical landscape effects)
Environment	Topography studies, river flows, dams, spillways, pollution studies
Sales	Convention sales, backdrops, booths
Law	Courtroom models
Museums and parks	Caves, physics demonstrations, period rooms, artifacts, planetariums, historical sites
Aeronautics	Wind resistance studies, destructive testing, displays, training films
Energy	Coal handling, solar energy systems
Amusement parks	Rides, park layouts
Underseas and naval	Water resistance studies, internal piping layouts, human environments, harbor studies
Medicine and science	Human and animal anatomy, molecular models
Prototypes	Patent applications, tests

Books About Modelmaking

Airplanes

Marmo, Richard. *Building Plastic Model Aircraft.* Tab Books, 1990.

Musciano, Walter. *Complete Book of Building and Flying Model Airplanes.* Prentice-Hall, 1986.

Weiss, Harvey. *Model Airplanes and How to Build Them.* Crowell, 1975.

Williams, Ron. *Building and Flying Indoor Model Airplanes.* Simon and Schuster, 1981.

Winter, William. *World of Model Airplanes.* Scribner, 1983.

Automobiles

Doty, Dennis. *Model Car Building.* Tab Books, 1989.

Hertz, Louis Heilbroner. *Complete Book of Building and Collecting Model Automobiles.* Crown, 1970.

Trench, Patrick. *Model Cars and Road Vehicles.* Pelham, 1983.

Weiss, Harvey. *Model Cars and Trucks and How to Build Them.* Crowell, 1989.

Railroading

Schleicher, Robert H. *Model Railroading Handbook.* Chilton, 1975.

Weiss, Harvey. *How to Run a Railroad: Everything You Need to Know About Model Trains.* Crowell, 1983.

Williams, Guy R. *World of Model Trains.* Putnam, 1970.

Ships

Johnson, Gene. *Model Ship Building.* 3d edition. Cornell Maritime, 1961.

Lozier, Herbert. *Model Boat Building.* Sterling, 1970.

Nordner, William. *How to Build Model Ships.* Hawthorne, 1969.

Weiss, Harvey. *Ship Models and How to Build Them.* Crowell, 1973.

Williams, Guy R. *World of Model Ships and Boats.* Deutsch, 1971.

Spacecraft

Olney, Ross R. *Out to Launch: Model Rockets.* Lothrop, 1979.

Ross, Frank. *Model Satellites and Spacecraft: Their Stories and How to Build Them.* Lothrop, 1969.

Stine, G. Harry. *Handbook of Model Rocketry.* 5th edition. Follett, 1983.

———. *New Model Rocketry Manual.* Arco, 1977.

Yates, Raymond Frances. *Model Jets and Rockets for Boys.* Harper, 1952.

General

Adkins, Jan. *Toolchest: A Primer of Woodcraft.* Walker, 1973.

Dean, William Albert. *Bill Dean's Book of Balsa Models.* Arco, 1970.

Frank, Adolph F. *Animated Scale Models Handbook.* Arco, 1981.

Jackson, Albert, and David Day. *The Modelmaker's Handbook.* Knopf, 1981.

Lozier, Herbert. *Getting Started in Model-Building.* Hawthorne, 1971.

Maginley, C. J. *Models of America's Past and How to Make Them.* Harcourt, Brace & World, 1969.

Meyer, Carolyn. *Saw, Hammer, and Paint—Woodworking and Finishing for Beginners.* Morrow, 1973.

Price, Brick. *The Model-Building Handbook.* Chilton, 1981.

Wagner, Willis H. *Modern Woodworking.* Goodheart-Wilcox, 1986.

Warring, Ron. *Balsa Wood Modeling.* Sterling, 1973.

Weiss, Harvey. *Machines and How They Work.* Crowell, 1983.

———. *Hammer and Saw.* Crowell, 1981.

———. *How to Be an Inventor.* Crowell, 1980.

———. *Model Buildings and How to Make Them.* Crowell, 1979.

———. *Working with Cardboard and Paper.* Addison-Wesley, 1978.

Weiss, Peter. *Scrap Wood Craft.* Lothrop, 1977.

Magazines

Finescale Modeler, Kalmbach Publishing Co., 1027 North Seventh Street, Milwaukee, WI 53233-1471.

Flying Models, Carstens Hobby Group, P.O. Box 700, Newton, NJ 07860.

Model Retailer, 14101-G Parke Long Court, Chantilly, VA 22110.

Model Shopper, 544 Second Street, San Francisco, CA 94107.

Railroad Model Craftsman, Carstens Hobby Group, P.O. Box 700, Newton, NJ 07860.

Scale Woodcraft, P.O. Box 510, Georgetown, CT 06829.

Acknowledgments

The Boy Scouts of America is grateful to the American Engineering Model Society, Walter A. Clothier, Sr., president, for their help in preparing the requirements and text for this revised edition of the *Model Design and Building* merit badge pamphlet. Members of the AEMS preparing this revision were James J. Iliff (committee chairman), Ward Pohl, Wendell Dunn, Roger Hammer, Don Rigling, Dave Wileman, Phil Brookshire, and Sherman Peeno.

The BSA also thanks Joe Paul Jones and Coy Veach of Freese and Nichols, Inc., Consulting Engineers, Fort Worth, Texas, for reviewing and suggesting improvements to the manuscript.

Notes

Notes

Notes

Notes

Notes

Notes